Encyclopædia Britannica

Fascinating Facts

Human Body

PUBLICATIONS INTERNATIONAL, LTD.

Louis Weber, C.E.O.
Publications International, Ltd.
7373 North Cicero Avenue
Lincolnwood, Illinois 60646

Printed in USA.

8 7 6 5 4 3 2 1

ISBN: 1-56173-317-2

A Special Kind of Muscle ▼

Hearts are made of a special kind of muscle that is found in no other part of the human body. This muscle has the power to relax and contract in a rhythm (the "lub-dub-lub-dub" sound you hear when you listen to your heartbeat). This expanding and contracting action pumps blood through the body's blood vessels.

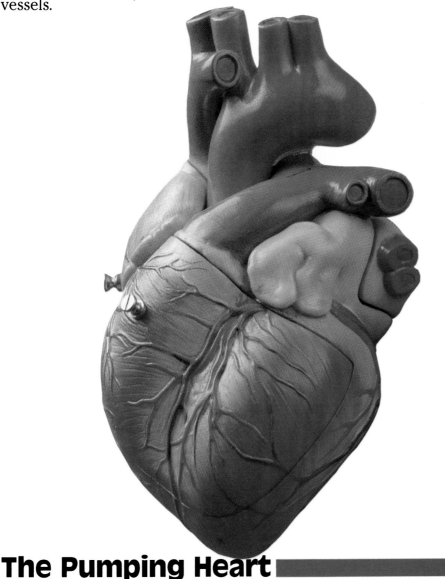

The Pumping Heart

The right side of your heart pumps blood through your lungs. That blood takes in oxygen, sending carbon dioxide back into the lungs to be breathed out. The oxygen is linked up with chemicals in the blood. This oxygen-rich blood then goes back to the left side of the heart, which pumps it out to the body.

The Heart of the Matter

Although some people are known as big-hearted, the size of a human heart depends on how large a person is, not on how nice or generous he or she is. The average adult heart weighs about 11 ounces (300 grams) and is about the size of a clenched fist.

Only a Heartbeat Away

When you are at rest, your heart beats about 70 times a minute—fast enough to send your entire blood supply through your body every minute. Here's how it works. Your body has about 8 to 10 pints (5 liters) of blood in it, and each beat of your heart sends about 2.5 ounces (50 ml) of blood out into your bloodstream. At a rate of 70 beats a minute, that works out to about 8 to 16 pints (5 to 8 liters) of blood moving through your body every minute. When you exercise, your heart beats faster—sometimes three times as fast as normal—to get more oxygen and nutrients to your hard-working muscles. When you sleep, your heart beats slower since your muscles need less oxygen.

Getting Energized

Blood is one of the busiest—and most important—parts of the body. First, it takes up the waste products that your body's tissues make as they work. Kidneys and other organs filter these waste products from the blood and turn them into urine that can be passed right out of the body. The blood also picks up the products of digestion—all the nutrients in your food—and takes them to the liver and other organs where they are turned into energy that helps you grow and work. Some of that energy is even stored away so that it is ready to be used when you are not eating.

Your Racing Heart ▲

Since the times of ancient Egyptians, people have believed that your heart is tied to your feelings. One reason for this is that your heart does react to what you do and how you feel. When you exercise or get excited, your heart works harder and beats faster. It also beats faster when you are frightened or angry. Illness makes your heart beat faster, too, so it can get fresh, oxygen-filled blood to your body. And, when you are rested and calm, your heart slows down.

Life-giving Oxygen

The cells in your body need oxygen to convert food into usable energy through chemical reactions. Without oxygen, the cells can't produce the energy, and they quickly die.

Heart Attacks are Serious

The official name for a heart attack is *myocardial infarction*. A small blood clot blocks one of the arteries that supply blood and oxygen to the heart muscle, causing part of the heart muscle to become damaged and die. The person having the heart attack may die without quick medical attention.

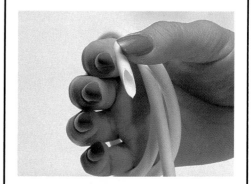

▲
Replacing Arteries

Recently, doctors have learned how to replace unhealthy arteries with healthy ones taken from other parts of the body—or even with ones made of plastic. This gives new hope for a better life to people whose arteries have become too narrow to give them enough oxygen-rich blood.

Blood-carrying Tubes ◀

Arteries and *veins* are both tubes that carry blood around your body. Arteries have very thick walls because they have to be strong enough to stand up to the pressures created by the heart as it pumps blood through them. They usually lie deep inside the tissues of your body, although in a few places they are near the surface of your skin—at your wrists, the side of your forehead, your neck, and even on the top and sides of your feet. Because the blood in the arteries is so filled with oxygen, arteries look bright red, the color of oxygen-rich blood. Veins, on the other hand, have much thinner walls because the blood inside them has lost much of the surging pressure it had when it first left the heart. They look blue because the blood in them is much darker after it sent oxygen out to the body. Veins bring blood safely back to the heart, which pumps it through the lungs to pick up more oxygen.

You Are What You Eat ▶

Bad food—food that has too much saturated fat, for example—can cause different kinds of problems. It can lead to "hardening of the arteries," in which arteries become clogged and gradually grow narrower, so that blood cannot pass through them properly. Eating too much bad food can also lead to obesity (being overweight) and high blood pressure, which can put great strain on a person's heart and cause disease and sometimes even death. This is why doctors urge people to avoid the kinds of fat in meat and fried foods and instead eat fruits and vegetables.

Massaging the Heart

When a heart stops working, it can sometimes be coaxed into working again. Doctors and paramedics massage the heart, for example, to try to get it to start its normal pumping action. They can also use electric shocks to make the heart muscle expand and contract—often, the heart begins working on its own again.

Pioneering Surgeon

Since the late 1960s, doctors have been able to remove a weak or diseased heart and replace it with a healthy organ. The first heart transplant was done by Dr. Christiaan Barnard in South Africa. Since then, doctors have perfected this operation.

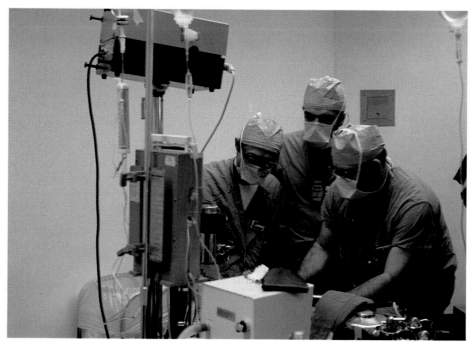

A Heart Transplant

During heart transplant surgery, a healthy heart is taken from a "donor," a person who has just died from something other than heart disease. The diseased heart is removed from the transplant patient and replaced with this new, healthy heart. The transplant is difficult, since the new heart has to match the new owner's blood, chemistry, and tissues. If it does not, the person's body may "reject" the new heart, and the person may die.

Regulating Your Heart Beat

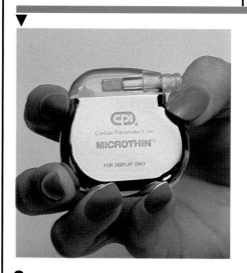

A *pacemaker* is a special device that helps control the speed at which a heart beats. Some people's hearts beat too slowly. To correct this, doctors insert a tiny wire into the wall of the heart. Small electric shocks—70 per minute—are given to the heart to keep the person's heart beating at exactly the right speed.

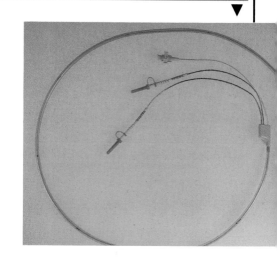

Our Body's Covering

Skin is a covering over the outside surface of humans that protects us from weather, injury, and germs. It is actually made up of three separate layers. The outermost layer, the one we see when we look at ourselves or another person, is called the "epidermis." It is made up of several kinds of cells. The middle layer is called the "dermis." It is much thicker than the outer layer, and it is made up of cells and fibers that are loosely woven together. Blood vessels, sweat glands, nerve endings, and the roots of our hair are all in the dermis. The inner layer is called the "subcutis." It is made up of fat that helps to cushion the organs in the body.

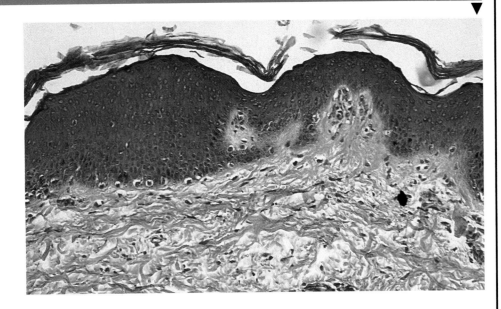

Giving Your Skin Color

Pigments, which give color to skin the same way they can give color to paint or crayons, are found in the epidermis. Actually, they are found in an inner layer of the epidermis called the "Malpighian layer," named after Marcello Malpighi, an Italian scientist who discovered it in the 1600s. Pigment makes people pale pink, red, yellow, brown, or black and causes freckles and suntans.

Leaving a Scar

When skin is cut or damaged in any way, the skin around it grows together to cover the injured area. Manually closing the gap made by the cut will make it easier for the new skin to grow, which is why bandages and stitches are used to "close" a cut. Sometimes, when this repairing process is not complete, a line is left without new skin. This is called a "scar."

Through Thick and Thin

Skin is thickest over the soles of our feet, a place that is exposed to pressure, friction, temperature changes, and sharp objects. It is thinnest on the eyelids, where it does the delicate work of protecting our eyes.

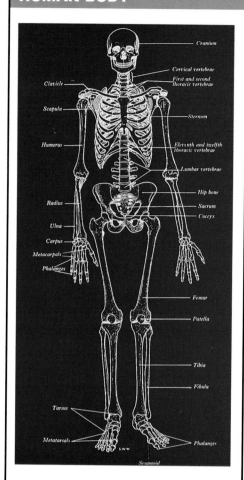

Hard as a Bone

Bone is a hard, grayish-white substance. Two-thirds is inorganic (mineral) matter, made up primarily of calcium in phosphate of lime, which gives it hardness. The remaining third is organic (animal) matter to give the bone toughness and a certain amount of flexibility that helps it not to break. About one-third of the weight of a bone is water.

Different Kinds of Bones ▼

Bone tissue is described as being compact (dense and smooth) or cancellous (resembling sponge inside). Humans and other mammals have four different shapes of bones: long bones, which are found in the limbs and are compact; short cancellous bones, such as those in the wrists and ankles; flat bones, which make up the skull; and irregular bones, such as those of the spine.

Inside a Bone

Some bones are hollow and are filled with a substance called marrow. The marrow is yellow and fatty in the long bones of adults. In other bones, the marrow is red and is filled with the red and white blood cells. There are also tiny passages or canals in compact bone. These carry blood, lymph (a watery fluid), and nerves through the bone, since bone is a living, highly active tissue.

A Very Tough ▲ Skeleton ▬

There are a total of 206 bones that make up the human skeleton. Together they form a supporting and protective framework for the body that is nearly as tough as cast iron yet less than half the weight.

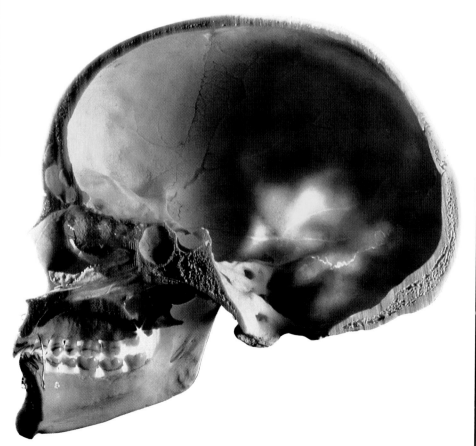

Using Your Joints▸

A joint is formed at the point where two separate bones meet. It is at these points that movement can take place. There are basically two types of joints. "Hinge" joints are found in the fingers, toes, knees, and elbows. They are simple joints that work like hinges. "Ball and socket" joints, found in the shoulders and hips, have large bones fitting into a socket. This type of joint offers a very wide range of movement.

Uses for Animal Bones

Animal bones are often treated chemically to prepare them for the making of different products. Among the uses for animal bones are fertilizer (artificial manure), gelatin, glue, and bone ash.

Holding Bones in Place

Ligaments are the strong bands of fiberlike tissues that hold two bones close together at a joint. They prevent a joint from moving too far and damaging the tissue inside. The strongest ligaments in the body are at the hip joint.

Healing a Broken Bone

A fractured bone must be set. This is done by placing the broken ends together so as to get the bone into its normal position. A sling or splint is then applied to let the bone knit. During this process, tiny cells known as *osteoblasts* produce a substance that makes the bones hard and firm again. These cells also help in natural growth. Other cells called *osteoclasts* tear down old bone tissue. This double process of building up and tearing down goes on in the bones all the time.

◂Broken Bones

A broken bone is called a fracture. Fractures can be of several different kinds, the two main types being simple and compound. In a compound fracture, the tissues of the body are torn and the bone is exposed to the open air. This is a very serious injury, since blood is lost and there is danger of infection. A simple fracture is one where the bone is broken but there is no wound.

Getting Rid of Dead Skin

The epidermis is actually made up of several layers of cells. New skin cells are created in the innermost layer and gradually work their way to the surface. As they reach the outer layers, they die. These dead cells are constantly being rubbed away every time your skin brushes against your clothing, your hands, or even the sheets you sleep on at night.

Working Up a Good Sweat

Sweat helps control our body's temperature. In our skin are coiled tubes called "sweat glands." Each of these opens onto the outer surface of the skin through a tiny hole called a "pore." The sweat that comes through our pores is made up of water and our body's waste products. As the water evaporates, it draws heat away and keeps our body's temperature in a safe range.

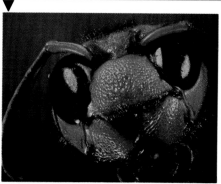

An insect has a very simple brain.

Using Your Brain

All animals have brains. Snails, worms, and other simple creatures have only a thickened nerve for a brain. More sophisticated animals need more complicated brains in order to control and carry out all of their different functions. Because we do more than any other kind of animal, the human brain is the most complicated. But it is made of the same materials and controls the same functions as the brains of many other animals.

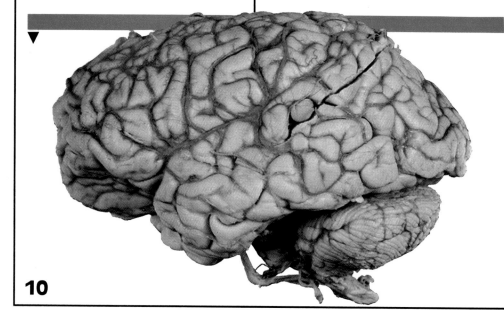

The Control Center

The brain is the source of what we know about the world. It is the center of our intelligence, our memory, our personality, and our awareness of the world around us. It is the brain that tells us what our eyes are seeing and what our ears are hearing. The brain controls our breathing, our digestion, and all the other activities that go on inside our bodies. It is the brain that solves math problems and remembers the punch line to a funny joke. The brain also controls what we do with our bodies—from walking and sleeping to talking and sneezing.

All Sorts of Brain Cells

The human brain is made of millions of tiny nerve cells called "neurons." Some are long and carry information to the different parts of our bodies through the spinal cord. Others are shorter and connect the different parts of the brain together.

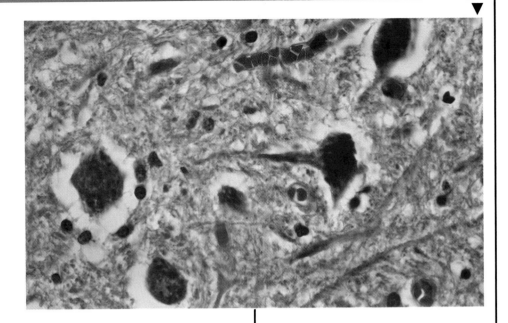

Listening to Your Brain

The cerebrum is the part of the brain that deals with feelings, thoughts, and awarenesses, letting us know, for example, that something feels hot and what hot means. Then, the cerebrum sends out instructions telling the body—or even another part of the brain—what to do about this information. Those instructions can be anything from telling our finger to get away from a hot match to informing another part of the brain to make our mouth and tongue say certain words.

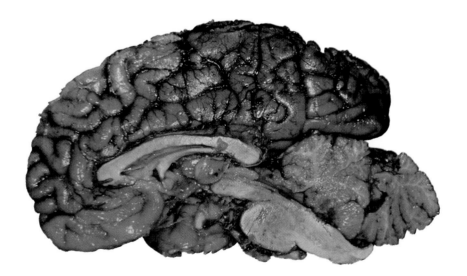

The Largest Part of the Brain

The part of the brain that deals with our thoughts, emotions, and personality is the *cerebrum*, which is the largest part of our brain. The cerebrum is so large that it must be wrinkled and creased in order to fit inside our skull. (If you took the cerebrum out of the skull and spread it out flat, it would be the size of a pillowcase.)

A Place for Everything

The cerebrum is carefully organized, so that control of each of our senses goes on in a particular part of the brain. The cells that control vision, for example, are located in the back part of the brain. The cells that control speaking are closer to the front of the brain. Each of these areas is linked to others so that the cerebrum can get complete information on what is happening throughout our body.

A Very Structured Brain

You might not believe it, but the areas of the cerebrum that control faster and more delicate movements are larger in size than those that control other movements. Since our hands often need to make fine, rapid movements, there is a large part of the cerebrum set aside for maneuvering our hands. Since the ankle and foot seldom make fine movements, there is only a small area set aside for controlling them.

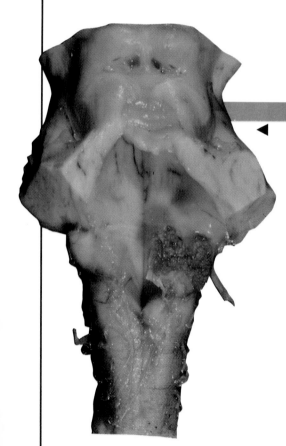

The Brain Connector

The *brain stem* connects the brain to the spinal cord and the rest of the body. It contains nerve fibers that control the body's internal organs—the lungs, liver, stomach, kidneys, and so on. It also controls the speed at which our heart beats and at which we breathe.

Having a Headache

Strangely enough, in spite of all the nerve cells inside the brain, the brain has no sensory nerves of its own. It cannot feel either pleasure or pain. What we call a "headache" actually comes from the membranes and tissues around the brain or from the muscles of the scalp, neck, or face.

Letting the Light in

An Eye Like a Camera

Like a camera, your eye has an opening that can adjust from one size to another. This opening is the *pupil*, the dark spot in the center of your eye. The eye also has a sensitive "film" on which the image of objects outside the eye are detected. The "film" is the *retina*, which is made up of cells that turn light rays into electrical signals that go to the brain to tell you what you are seeing.

The circle of color and the dark spot in the very middle of the eye are the *iris* and the *pupil.* The pupil lets light into the eye. The iris controls the amount of light coming in by changing the size of the pupil—just like the shutter that opens and closes inside a camera. In bright light, the tiny muscles inside the iris can close the pupil to the size of a tiny pinhole. In darkness, the iris opens the pupil up so that more light can get in.

A Round and Firm Eye

Vitreous humor is a jellylike substance inside the eye that helps keep the eye round and firm. Without it, the eye would get out of shape, collapse, and become totally useless.

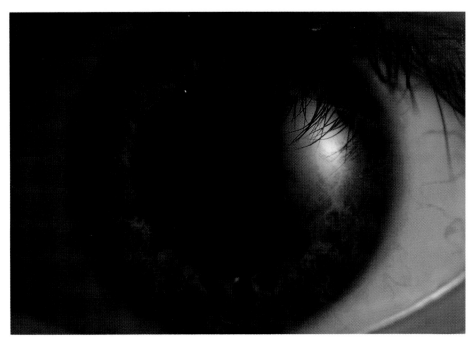

Straight into the Eye

The pupil has no color at all. It looks black because it opens directly onto the inside of the eye. When you see a black pupil, you are looking straight through to what is in the eye itself.

Seeing the World Around Us

Light entering the eye makes its way to the retina—the "film" at the back of the eye's camera. Once the light has been turned into electrical signals and sent to the brain, the brain takes over. It sorts out the signals and relates them to familiar objects, colors, shapes, and other features. It is actually the brain that lets us see.

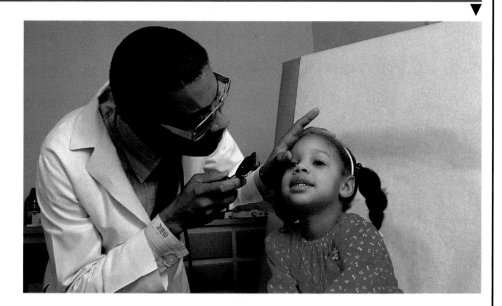

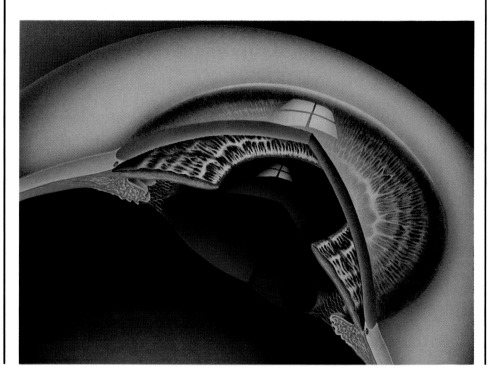

In Living Color

The *rods* and *cones* are the two kinds of cells inside the retina. (Remember, the retina is the "film" at the back of the eye that receives the image of what is outside.) The rods detect light—and they see only in black and white. The cones see colors. However, they are not as sensitive, and they work well only in bright light. As a result, we tend to see only in different shades of gray when someone turns off the lights.

Blinking the Dust Away

Blinking is a *reflex*—something that happens automatically without our control. It helps to keep our eyes clean. Each time you blink, you clear away dust, dirt, and anything else that might have gotten onto the surface of your eye. It also helps to keep unwanted objects out of the eye.

Cleansing Tears ◀

Tears are not just a sign of being sad or upset. They are an important part of seeing because tears help wash away dust, germs, or dirt that get into your eyes. The tear glands at the upper, outer part of your eye socket release small amounts of this salty liquid. After tears have collected this dust and dirt, they make their way to your *tear ducts*, which are little tubes on the inner side of your eye socket near your nose. The tears go through the tear ducts into two sacs, which drain into your nasal cavities. They take the dirt, dust, and germs with them as they go. When your eyes are tearing heavily, tears may also drip down your face.

Animal Eyes

Animals with backbones tend to have eyes much the same as ours. Some of them can see even better than we do—hawks, eagles, and other birds of prey, for example.

Compound Eyes of Insects

Insects have a completely different kind of eye than people do. Their eye is called a "compound" eye. It contains many tiny lenses clustered together, much like a honeycomb. Worker bees, for example, have up to 5,000 of these tiny lenses in each eye. Each lens detects a small part of the scene. The insect's brain puts together all of these thousands of tiny pictures to see what is going on.

Through Baby's Eyes

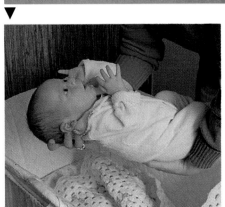

A newborn baby can see, but cannot clearly see things that are far away. He or she can detect changes in brightness, contrast, and movement. The newborn will stare intently at his or her mother's face when she brings it close to his or hers. After about two weeks, the infant will look at large objects with interest. By about eight to ten weeks of age, the newborn will use his or her eyes to follow an object that is passed in front of his or her face.

Curing a Wandering Eye

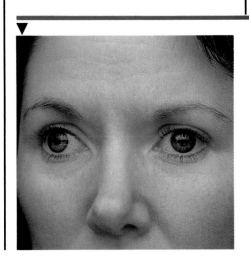

In order to see properly, both of your eyes must work together. They must both be able to focus on the same object at the same time. Then, they can relay their signals to the brain, which translates the two signals (one from each eye) into a single, three-dimensional image. Sometimes, the eyes of babies or young adults do not point in the same direction. This condition is called *strabismus.* One eye may be turned inward (called "cross eye") or it may point upward (called "wall-eye"). This problem can often be corrected by a doctor through the use of an eye patch, eye drops, or special muscle exercises. Surgery to adjust the length of the muscles that move the eye may also be used. If the condition is not corrected early, the brain may begin to ignore the signals coming from the wandering eye, and permanent vision damage may result. This condition is called *amblyopia* or "lazy eye."

Nose Jobs

Besides helping us smell, the nose is one of the links between the outside air and the blood that takes oxygen to all the different parts of your body. Your nostrils take in the air, filter out dirt and grit, and pass it inside. Inside the nose, mucous membranes covered with tiny hairs sweep the dust and germs toward the nostrils to be sneezed out or toward the back of the nose to be swallowed, where stomach acid will eliminate them. Blood vessels inside the nose warm the air so that, before it goes on to your lungs, it has been warmed, filtered, and even moistened.

What a Nice Smell

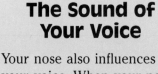

Odors are detected by two small areas at the top of your nose called the "olfactory epithelium." These areas, which are outgrowths of the brain, are filled with nerve cells. As smells are breathed in from the air, their small particles are dissolved in the mucous lining. A reaction is caused in certain cells, depending on what odor is present. Our nose helps us to identify thousands of different smells.

The Sound of Your Voice

Your nose also influences your voice. When your nose is clogged, the sound of your voice changes. The size and shape of a person's nose can also affect his or her voice.

A Keen Sense of Hearing

Even though the human ear is a first-rate device for hearing, certain animals have better hearing. Dogs and wild animals, for example, can hear much softer, fainter sounds than we can, while bats can hear high-pitched sounds that people cannot hear at all.

Anatomy of an Ear

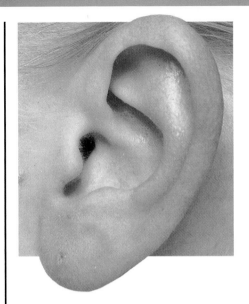

Human ears actually have three parts. The outer ear (the part that sticks out a bit from the side of your head), or "auricle," is a flap of skin and gristle that protects the rest of the ear and funnels sound into the ear. It contains a short tube whose inner end is closed by a tiny membrane called the "eardrum." Just beyond this is the middle ear, which is a small space that holds three small bones. Behind this is another tube, called the "Eustachian tube," which runs to the back of the nose and helps to keep the proper air pressure within the middle ear. The middle ear is connected to the inner ear by the oval window, which is covered by the base of one of the inner ear bones.

Sorting Out the Noise

The brain plays an important part in hearing. Once the sound waves are turned into electrical signals and are sent to the brain, the brain identifies whether the sounds are high-pitched or low-pitched and whether they are loud or soft. If several sounds are heard at the same time, the brain sorts them out so you can concentrate on one of them at a time. Then, it identifies the sound—recognizing what it is, exactly who is speaking, what song is being sung, or whatever. It is a complicated job, but one that takes our brain just a fraction of a second to carry out.

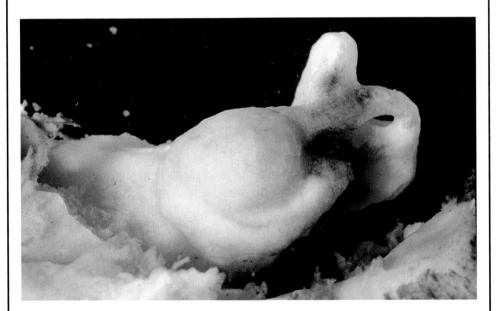

Functions of the Inner Ear

The most important part of the inner ear for hearing is the *cochlea*, which is shaped like the shell of a snail. Inside it are fluid and tiny hairs. When vibrations reach the inner ear, they are caught by this fluid and passed on to the hairs, which are stimulated to produce nerve signals. These signals are then carried by the auditory nerve to the brain.

Very Little Ear Bones

The hammer, the anvil, and the stirrup are the three small bones in the middle ear that magnify the vibrations that are made as sound waves strike the eardrum. These vibrations are then passed on to the inner ear, where they are translated into nerve signals and sent to the brain.

Responding to the World

In human beings, the nervous system is controlled by the brain and the spinal cord, which together make up the central nervous system. The central nervous system receives information from and sends out instructions to the body through a network of small nerves called the peripheral nervous system. With these two systems—the central and peripheral—the body knows what is going on around it and can respond to any changes. This is the same type of nervous system that other mammals have. In contrast, human beings have a brain whose function is to deal with thinking, memory, emotions, and all the other things that make up the human personality and intelligence.

Fast Nerve Impulses

Each individual peripheral nerve is a bundle of thousands of very small nerve cells called *neurones.* Each neurone has a central nerve fiber (axon) surrounded by an insulating nerve sheath (myelin), and every neurone has its own cell body that controls the chemical reactions of the cell. Information is carried as a small electrical current along the axon. The myelin sheath prevents the nerve impulse from leaking out and speeds up the impulse to over 164 feet (50 m) a second.

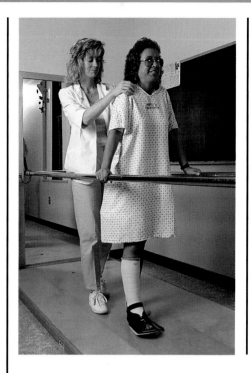

Unusual Body Cells

As body cells, neurones are unusual. Once damaged, they are rarely able to mend themselves. However, by using other, undamaged nerve pathways, the affected person can often make a good recovery.

An Automatic Nervous System▾

The nervous system also controls the workings of all the internal body organs. For example, the brain affects the speed of the heartbeat and the workings of the intestines. We are not aware that this control is happening. It is automatic and is performed by a separate network of nerves called the automatic nervous system.

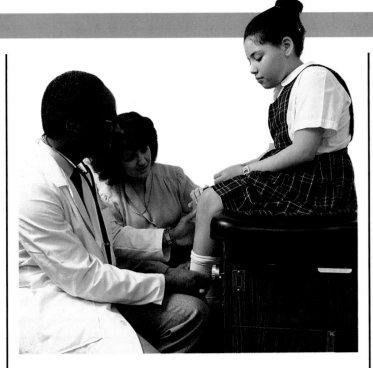

A Very Common Reflex ▲

An example of a reflex is a muscle stretch reflex. If you sit relaxed with one leg crossed over the other and sharply tap the knee just below the kneecap, the leg will jerk as the thigh muscles contract. In this reflex, the sensory nerves in the thigh muscles detect a slight stretch of the muscle when you tap the knee. This is converted into a nerve impulse that travels to the spinal cord, which tells the muscle of the thigh to contract to overcome the stretch. This particular reflex is not under the control of the brain and is called a spinal reflex.

Running the Automatic Nervous System

The hypothalamus at the base of the brain runs the automatic nervous system. It sends impulses to control the vital body functions of the heart, lungs, kidneys, intestines, and bladder. The hypothalamus also controls the production of chemical substances called hormones, which circulate around the body in the bloodstream. They control the many biochemical processes and also the way in which we grow and develop.

Walking Across the Room

In addition to the activities that go on without our knowing, the brain allows us to carry out actions whenever we want. This is called voluntary activity. For example, if you decide to walk across the room, your brain will organize the muscles needed to perform these movements.

Difficult to Understand ▲

The most difficult feature of the nervous system to understand is the control of our emotions and personality. These are called higher nervous functions. They enable us to overcome our instincts and reflexes—for example, to sacrifice our own safety.

19

A Real Balancing Act

One of the most important jobs of the ear has nothing to do with hearing—the ear helps us to keep our balance. Inside the inner ear are three canals, all shaped like half-circles. These canals are filled with fluid, and, together with sight, they help the brain to detect the body's movement and the position of the head, giving us a sense of balance. Infections and disorders in these canals can cause dizziness and difficulty in walking.

Smelling the Taste

A great deal of what you taste is actually a matter of smell. To test this, try eating something when you have a cold or when you are holding your nose. (Remember when you did this whenever you had to eat something you didn't like?) You'll find that what you eat seems almost tasteless, simply because you cannot smell it.

The Sense of Taste

Taste buds are little taste detectors in the mouth. Most of them are on the tongue, but a few are scattered around the inside of the mouth and the back of the throat.

Learning About Food

All children seem to be fussy eaters. They are learning what food they like and dislike and are trying to convince grownups to give them only the foods they like best.

Four Basic Tastes

Believe it or not, all tastes—from apple pie to your favorite burger and sauce—come from four basic tastes. These are salty, sour, sweet, and bitter. All the different flavors you get from what you eat and drink are just mixes of two or more of these main tastes.

Seeing Your Breath

Our bodies get rid of the air inside of us because much of it has been turned into carbon dioxide, which can be poisonous. So, we breathe the carbon dioxide back into the air outside. The air we exhale also contains quite a bit of water vapor from the moist lining in our lungs. On cold days, this vapor condenses into little drops of water as we exhale. When it comes in contact with the cold outside air, it forms the steam that comes from your mouth on a winter day.

Breathing for Life

When blood returns to the heart from its trip around your body, the heart pumps the blood through blood vessels in your lungs. The lungs are the main organs for breathing. Air comes into the lungs from the nose and throat. Oxygen from that air then passes through the thin lining inside of the lungs into the bloodstream. Carbon dioxide, which was picked up from tissues throughout the body, passes from the blood into the lungs. We then breathe the carbon dioxide out into the outside world.

Breathing Often

The air we breathe only contains about 20 percent oxygen. In order to get the oxygen we need, we have to breathe often.

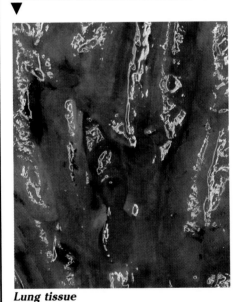

Lung tissue

Light and Airy

Lungs are light and spongy because they contain so much air. In fact, each of your two lungs weighs only about a pound (1/2 kg). They are also very elastic, stretching each time you breathe in and springing back to their normal shape when you breathe out.

Breathing Through a Mask

Many problems can be caused by breathing in harmful substances. There are many "dust diseases," for example, that affect miners, farmers, stone masons, and other people who work in dusty areas. Asbestos is another substance that can harm your lungs, as is tobacco. Many people who work in dangerous environments now wear masks, so that the dust and harmful poisons can be filtered out before reaching their lungs.

Lots of Air Bubbles

The body's main breathing tube is the windpipe, which runs through your throat. When it reaches the upper part of your chest, it divides. One main airway goes into each of your two lungs. Inside your lungs, these airways divide again and again, becoming smaller and smaller. They finally end in tiny air bubbles shaped like bunches of grapes. There are about 300 million of these tiny air bubbles in each of your lungs. Each time you breathe, air passes through the wind pipe, down the airway, and into these air bubbles. It is from these air bubbles that oxygen passes into your bloodstream.

Different-shaped Stomachs

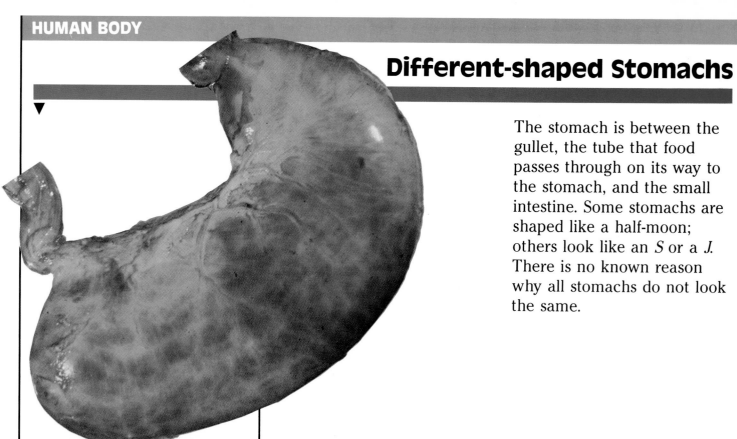

The stomach is between the gullet, the tube that food passes through on its way to the stomach, and the small intestine. Some stomachs are shaped like a half-moon; others look like an *S* or a *J*. There is no known reason why all stomachs do not look the same.

The Process of Digestion

As food passes into the upper part of the stomach, gastric juices break it up so that it can be absorbed in the small intestine. The food then moves to the middle of the stomach, where more digestion takes place. To mash and pulverize food, the stomach has three layers of muscles along its inside walls. Finally, the partly digested food goes to a narrow area, which acts as a kind of valve to control the rate at which the food passes into the small intestine.

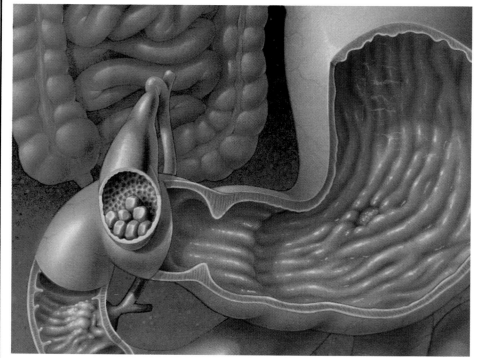

Putting Food in Your Stomach

Because your stomach churns food around and mixes it with enzymes and other gastric juices, it quickly turns your food—anything from pretzels and potato chips to steak or yogurt—into a thick, soupy liquid. Scientists and doctors call this liquid "chyme." When chyme is watery enough, it passes on to the small intestine, where it can be absorbed into your body.

No Digestion Needed ◄

Water, pure honey, and fruit sugars are absorbed by the body almost immediately. They pass through the stomach and into the small intestine with hardly any action on the part of the stomach.

That Burning Sensation

Heartburn is a burning sensation in the stomach that is caused when acidic, half-digested food backs up into the esophagus. This is most common when a person lies down or bends down after eating a big meal. Antacids and other medicines may relieve this uncomfortable feeling.

Working on Your Food

Your stomach is lined with millions of tiny glands that pour gastric juice on the food that enters your stomach. Your stomach mixes the food together so that these gastric juices get a good chance to "work" on the food. The juices themselves contain a lot of different things, including hydrochloric acid and enzymes. These enzymes help digest all the different kinds of food, from proteins to carbohydrates.

Digestion Time

How long it takes for digestion to take place varies, depending on what you ate and how much you ate. It takes longer to digest some foods than others—milk and lamb chops, for example, are much harder to digest than a glass of orange juice. Likewise, a big meal means more work—and a longer time—than a small snack.

An Upset Stomach

"Indigestion" is a word we use to cover a lot of different feelings and discomforts. It can be caused by an infection of bacteria or viruses or by eating foods—like beans, cucumbers, and other items—that introduce gas into the intestines. The discomfort usually passes within a few hours.

Ulcers Aren't Fun

An ulcer is a raw spot on the lining of a part of the digestive system—the stomach, the duodenum, or even both. Scientists are not sure exactly what causes ulcers.

23

The Growth of Hair

The hair on our heads grows about 2/5 inch a month (1 cm) or 5 inches (13 cm) a year. However, it hardly ever grows more than about 20 inches (51 cm) long because each hair lives for only three or four years. It then falls out and a new one starts growing at almost the same point to take its place.

Shorter Body Hairs▲

Our eyelashes and eyebrows and the little hairs on our skin grow more slowly than the hairs on our heads. They also have a much shorter life. For these two reasons they never grow very long.

Straight and Curly Hair

If you cut different hairs across and look at them through a microscope, you will see that some are rounder than others. The rounder a hair, the straighter it will be, and the flatter a hair, the more it will curl.

Different Amounts of Hair

▼

Among human beings, some Chinese have very little hair and almost no beards. The people called the Ainus of Japan are hairy almost all over.

No Hair at All

Babies are born with a covering of fine down, which is replaced with the usual growth of hair as the child grows older. This hairy coat is barely noticeable, since it consists of very fine hair that is light in color. However, a human being's skin is hairy almost everywhere except on the palms of the hands, soles of the feet, and the lips.

Growing Teeth

Most babies are born without teeth. First teeth appear at about six months. By the age of about two and a half, all of the 20 deciduous (milk, or first) teeth have appeared.

A Second Set of Teeth ▲

The permanent, or second, set of teeth forms in the gum below the first teeth and pushes them out as they grow up. There are 32 of these, 16 in each jaw. The eight at the front are cutting teeth called *incisors;* the next four are pointed teeth called *canines;* eight, the *premolars,* take the place of the earlier molars of the first teeth, and the back twelve, called *molars,* are grinding teeth.

Wise Third Molars

The permanent teeth appear between the ages of 6 and 14, except for the four "wisdom teeth" whose proper name is third molars. These do not appear until the ages of about 20 to 25, when people are supposed to have reached the years of wisdom. In some people, they never grow.

Tooth Decay ▲

The most common cause of toothache is caries, or decay. If teeth and gums are not properly cleaned, tiny pieces of food are left sticking to them. The sugar in food, bacteria, and the acids made by the bacteria cause the enamel to decay.

25

Muscle Action ◀

Muscles are the body's "movers," which control most of your actual actions. Without them, you would not be able to walk, eat, talk, or even breathe.

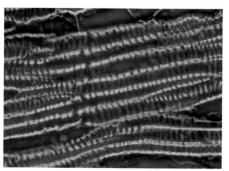

Cardiac muscle is only found in the heart.

Muscular Types ▲

There are three different types of muscles in your body. The first is *involuntary*, or smooth, muscle. The fibers of these muscles are made up of long, spindle-shaped cells that are pointed at each end. They are found in blood vessels and hollow organs, and they carry out the automatic functions of the body. The second type of muscles are the *voluntary* muscles. These are made up of bundles of long fibers, with each fiber connected to a nerve ending. Whenever a motor nerve receives a signal from the brain, it passes it on to the muscle fiber, which then contracts. When all of the fibers shorten at the same time, the muscle shortens. The third kind of muscle is the *cardiac* muscle, found only in the heart. Like the other two types of muscles, cardiac muscle has the ability to contract. But, cardiac muscle does not require a signal from the nervous system in order to contract. The heart has a built-in pacemaker that triggers the contractions that we call heartbeats.

Resting Tired Muscles ▼

When our body turns sugar into energy, it also produces lactic acid, which collects in the muscle that is being used and makes it feel tired. When the muscle is involved in a quick discharge of movement, the body may not be able to move the lactic acid quickly enough. The buildup may make the muscle so tired that it can do no more work until the lactic acid is removed. To get rid of the buildup of lactic acid, the body needs oxygen. This is one reason why you breathe heavier—and feel a need to rest—after running to catch a bus.

A runner covers his legs with a "space blanket" to keep warm after a race in order to avoid muscle cramping.

Let's Exercise

Muscles need exercise in order to remain elastic—bendable, movable, and strong. Without exercise, they begin to decrease in size. They may also become less efficient at the work they are designed to do. That's why it is so important for people—especially children—to exercise regularly.

Deep Sleep, Light Sleep ▼

Scientists know that there are two different kinds of sleep. REM sleep (REM stands for "rapid eye movement") is the period of sleep during which your eyes flicker rapidly and you dream. NREM (meaning non-REM) is divided into four progressively deeper stages of sleep. Although you may sleepwalk during NREM sleep, you generally do not dream. These two kinds of sleep alternate the whole time you are asleep. NREM sleep accounts for about 80 percent of your sleep time, while REM sleep accounts for about 20 percent.

Giving Your Body a Rest ▲

When you are asleep, you are unconscious—unaware of anything that is going on. You are also resting more completely than at any other time. During the time when you sleep, certain chemicals in your body get a chance to build up again, just as muscles and other parts get a chance to rest and rebuild their strength.

The Common Cold

The common cold is a viral illness of the upper respiratory system—the nose and throat. The usual symptoms are sneezing, stuffed or runny nose, watery eyes, aching, and scratchy throat. Earache, headache, and a fever are also possible.

Taking Aspirin

For high fever in adults, aspirin may be used. Parents, however, should consult a doctor *before* giving a child aspirin, because aspirin has been linked to a life-threatening childhood disease called Reye's syndrome.

A Cure for the Common Cold ▼

There isn't any way to cure a cold. Your body simply builds up *antibodies*, special forces that act against the viral infection, and the cold just goes away. Rest and drinking plenty of fluids help your body fight back.

A child with a cold is having his temperature taken in the armpit.

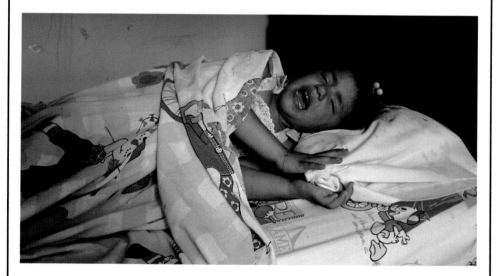

In Bed with the Flu

Influenza, better known as the flu, is a more serious viral infection, usually of the nose, throat, and lungs. Flu symptoms may include high fever, chills, cough, headache, sore throat, muscular aches, and weakness. Stuffy nose, diarrhea, and vomiting are also possible. In mild cases, most symptoms disappear in about five days. Sometimes, however, the body's weakened condition can lead to other infections, including pneumonia. Rest and drinking plenty of fluids are essential as the body fights the infection.

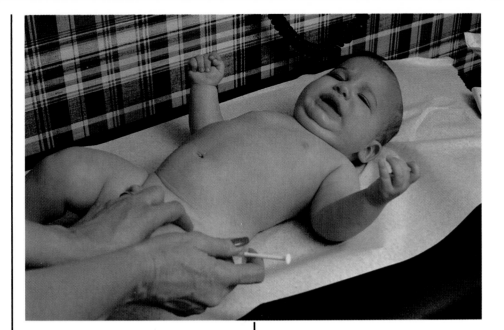

Vaccines to Combat the Flu ◀

A flu vaccine works by causing the body to produce antibodies to fight against a specific influenza virus. The biggest problem is that flu viruses keep changing. As soon as a vaccine is developed that works against one type of flu virus, the virus changes a little and the vaccine no longer works. Even so, certain groups of people who have a higher risk of complications, such as the elderly, may be advised to get a flu shot.

Passing It Along ▲

One reason that measles and German measles spread so quickly is that they are caught by being exposed to someone else's sneezes or coughs. Another reason is that parents often think that the disease is over once the fever is gone (but before the red spots or rash appear), and they send their children back to school. Unfortunately, the children still have the disease at this point, and they end up passing it on to many other children at their school.

Miserable Measles

Measles, also called *rubeola*, is one of the most widespread diseases of all. It is caused by a virus and can be spread from person to person by sneezes and coughs. It begins in the nose and throat like a cold; a high temperature follows. Three to five days later, red spots appear on the skin of the face, ears, and neck. They spread all over the body and last for about four days. Once you've had measles, you will not catch it again. Measles can be prevented through vaccination in childhood.

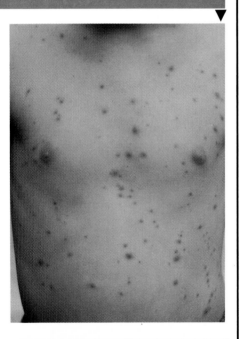

Catching German Measles

German measles, usually called *rubella,* is a mild viral infection. Symptoms include fever, swollen glands, joint pain, and a pink or red rash on the face and body. German measles are not dangerous to most people except pregnant women. If a pregnant woman catches the infection, her baby may be born with birth defects, for example, deafness. Vaccination in childhood is encouraged mainly to keep children from catching German measles and spreading it to pregnant women.

Pretty Much Under Control

Tuberculosis, or TB, is a disease caused by a tiny, rod-shaped germ that is spread in the air when a TB victim coughs. It can also be spread by a germ that lives in the milk of cows that have the disease. Tuberculosis can be very dangerous—years ago, patients who had it simply wasted away and died. Today, tuberculosis is rare in the United States.

Combatting a Killer

In the United States today, advances have been made in the detection and treatment of tuberculosis. Simple skin tests can be given to people who are suspected of having the disease or who are at risk of having it. Those who are at risk can be given a vaccine called BCG. In this country and in many others, cows are tested regularly to prevent dangerous, TB-infected milk from reaching the public. Milk is treated with a special process called "pasteurization" to kill the deadly germs before it is sold.

Sick with the Mumps

Mumps, like measles, is caused by a virus, and there is very little you can do to get rid of it. The illness begins with a fever, neck pain, headache, and weakness. A day or two later, the glands in the neck begin to swell and it becomes hard to open the mouth or swallow. After four or five days, the temperature and swelling go down. All you can do for mumps is to stay in bed and eat whatever you can swallow. Mumps is not usually a serious condition, although the risk of complications appears to be somewhat higher in adults who catch it.

A Very Nasty Virus

Poliomyelitis, or polio for short, is another disease caused by a virus. It usually affects children and young adults, and it is generally caught by either being in contact with someone who has polio or by being in an area with poor health standards. The disease begins with a fever, a sore throat, and vomiting. In most cases, the disease is fairly mild. It can, however, attack the nervous system and spine, leaving the patient partially or even fully paralyzed. Polio can be prevented through a series of vaccinations. Vaccination has made polio rare in the United States today.

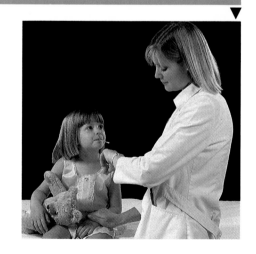

The Second-leading Cause of Death ▼

Cancer is the name we give to a whole group of diseases in which strange lumps occur and spread into other parts of the body. No one knows exactly what causes cancer, but it seems to be linked to abnormal growth patterns in cells. Removal of the lumps, radiation, and treatment with chemicals are used to treat cancer once it is found. Cancer is the second-leading cause of death in Western countries.

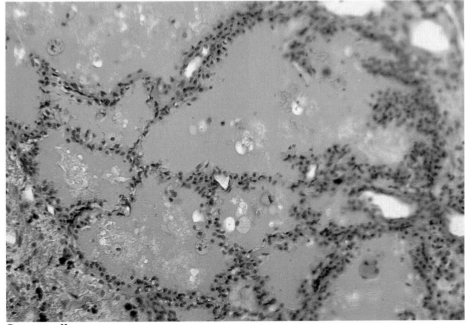

Cancer cells

A Disease Carried by Mosquitoes

Malaria is one of the most common diseases in tropical areas. It brings on high, violent fevers in which a person feels unbearably cold and then, terribly hot. It is spread by mosquitoes, which deposit the germ directly into a person's blood when he or she is bitten. The best way to prevent malaria is to get rid of mosquitoes by draining swamps and mosquito breeding grounds and by using insecticides. People who travel in areas where malaria is common can also take certain drugs to help prevent the disease.

A bite from an infected mosquito can result in malaria.